THE SEVEN SPIRITS OF LORD

Chelsea Kong

© 2023-2024 Chelsea Kong

All rights reserved. All images used in this book are licensed copies from their respectful owners including myself, Canva, Unsplash, Pixabay and Pexels. This book or any portion thereof may not be reproduced or used in any manner whatsoever without the express written permission of the publisher except for the use of brief quotations in a book review.

Printed in 2024, Made in Toronto, Canada
ISBN: 978-1-990399-63-3
Library and Archives Canada

The spirit of the Lord

spirit of wisdom

spirit of understanding

The Lord will let you know things. You will know secrets.

I AM Strong

spirit of counsel and might

Pray

spirit of the fear (awe) of the Lord

Be in awe of the Lord and you will walk in victory.

Pray, worship, read the Bible, go to church.

Walk in love.

Tell others what Jesus tells you to say to them.

SALVATION PRAYER

God, I know I sinned against you. Forgive me for the wrong that I have done. I believe that Jesus Christ died on the cross for me. That He rose from the grave so that after three days. I can have His long-lasting life. Come into my heart to be my Lord and Savior. I choose to turn away from my sins and I choose to follow you. Lead me to walk with you. Keep me safe and teach me your ways. Stop every bad thing in my life that has an open door to hurt me. Close those doors. Holy Spirit fill me now in Jesus' name. Amen.

BAPTISM IN THE HOLY SPIRIT

Jesus, you are the one that fills me with Your Spirit. Come Holy Spirit and come into my life and fill me to overflow with Your presence. Come with your fire too. Thank you for the gift of tongues in Jesus' name. Amen.

Open your mouth and let the words come out that God gives you. It will be words that you don't know what they mean. You can ask God what it means. You need to let Him talk through you every day to grow this gift.

He will bring you closer to God and you will know Jesus more. You will have power from God to do great things and know things.

PRAYER

Thank you, Father God, for teaching me about. The seven spirits of God. I want to have the seven spirits of God. Teach me how to walk in. Your ways and live with the fear of God. I want to obey you all the days of my life. Make me strong for you. I want to go with you, Jesus. I want to walk in your power and by the Holy Spirit in Jesus' name. Amen.

Message from the Author

The fear of the Lord is the secret to walking in God's power. We will have victory when we have the fear of the Lord. We need to remember that God is holy and to obey Him all the time. We need to know how to use the gifts of the Holy Spirit right. The Holy Spirit gives us the gifts to help others. We must honour Him. Holy Spirit will tell us God's word for others. We need to let them know they are from God. This pleases God and keeps us safe from pride and trouble. The devil wants to destroy us. He will do everything that he can to make trouble for us.

OTHER PRODUCTS

- Knowing God
- How to Hear God's Voice
- New Life in Jesus
- Loving Israel
- God's Gifts/Spiritual Talents
- Meeting God
- Word Power
- Fruit of the Spirit
- The Tabernacle
- Bride for Jesus
- A Life of Prayer
- Live Free
- Who am I in Jesus
- Walk in Love
- God's Favor
- Man of God
- Woman of God
- How to Use Money
- God's Wisdom
- Fasting
- See Jerusalem and Bethany
- First Fruit Offering
- Feast of Trumpets
- Day of Atonement
- Feast of Tabernacles
- Counting the Omer
- Festival of Lights
- Glory, Presence, and Holy Spirit
- Live in God's Presence
- Pentecost
- See Galilee, Nazareth, and Tiberias
- Hear God Speak
- Knowing Jesus
- Knowing Holy Spirit
- A Healthy Life and Healthy Life Work Book
- Smokey the Cat
- Passover Unleavened Bread
- Resurrection Life
- Proverbs 31 Woman
- Loving Jesus
- The Blessing
- Revival
- Chelsea Learns Hebrew
- Thanksgiving
- Give Thanks
- Jesus Birth

OTHER PRODUCTS

Loving Jesus: Bride and Groom
Proverbs 31 Woman
Colours in the Bible
Breakthroughs
Open Doors

Coming soon
ABCs of Faith
An Eagle's Life

Teaching Series
How to Hear God's Voice Teaching Guide & Audio Book
Relationship with God, Jesus, Holy Spirit Guide
Knowing God, Jesus, Holy Spirit Guide & Audio Book
Flowing in the Prophetic

Teaching (Non-Sale on my website)
Purim
Passover
Resurrection

More books to come!

Devotionals
31 Day Devotional

Inspirational/Other
Chelsea's Psalms and Poems
Your Daily Meal: Chelsea's Photo Album

Puzzle Books
Biblical Puzzle Book Vol 1-5
Bible Puzzles for Young Children Book 1-3
Biblical Puzzle for Children Books 1-5

BOOK REVIEWS

More books on Amazon, Kobo, and Barnes and Noble, Smashwords, and IngramSpark.
https://chelseak532002550.wordpress.com/

> More books on Amazon, Kobo, and Barnes and Noble, Smashwords, and IngramSpark.
> https://www.amazon.com/author/chelseakong
>
> Please leave a review and share with friends to help the author continue to write more books to reach more readers. Thank you so much for your support.

Review!

About
CHELSEA KONG

She is a writer, creative arts and digital media artist, skilled administration professional, and podcaster. Chelsea also served in a variety of roles, from audiovisual, photography, to assisting on the worship team, and ministry team. She also has a passion for families being united.

Chelsea has been a guest on Unity Live Radio and The Lady Tracey Show and is highly recommended by a Proud Christian blog. She graduated from Hotel and Restaurant Management, Digital Media Arts, Office Administration, and experience working with children. Chelsea lives in Toronto, Canada. She mainly writes children's books, stories, bridal writing, poems, lyrics for songs, words of encouragement, blessings, prayers, and jokes. The author of How to Hear the Voice of God, the Bridal Collection, Knowing God, etc. She also has her own Bible Puzzle books and other inspired products. Her podcast channel is called Chelsea K on Anchor, Spotify, and iTunes.

Please check my website to find out more:
https://chelseak532002550.wordpress.com/

www.ingramcontent.com/pod-product-compliance
Lightning Source LLC
LaVergne TN
LVHW072118070426
835510LV00003B/120